d"

DO NOT REMOVE
CARDS FROM POCKET

6/25/93

ALLEN COUNTY PUBLIC LIBRARY
FORT WAYNE, INDIANA 46802

You may return this book to any agency, branch,
or bookmobile of the Allen County Public Library.

DEMCO

FEEL SAFE ANYWHERE
"You Can Be Your Own Bodyguard"

For information write to: J. R. Moore
Tiger Enterprises
PO Box 9901
St. Louis, Missouri 63122 (USA)

First Edition
ISBN: 0-9633458-0-X

Library of Congress Catalog Card Number: 92-61239

Designed and Typeset by:
K-A-V Publishing Company
(a division of)
Ancona & Associates, Inc.
(314) 394-2019

Printed in the United States of America

ACKNOWLEDGEMENTS

This book is dedicated to Hilda Kaufmann my high school english instructor, who first saw a spark of writing talent more than 26 years ago.

I owe much to my friend, mentor and business advisor Joe A. Steinmetz. To my wife Mary Ann, who has stood by me, encouraged me, proof reads my work and is my best friend. To Joe Ancona who motivated me to start writing. To G. L. Y. who initially was asked to review the book and whose help has contributed so much. To Chester Ditch for his update on police equipment.

To my friend, artist Gary Bemis for his creative cover art: Kerr House Studios, Mr. Gary Bemis, 314-629-3646

Each chapter starts with a quote from The Art of War, by Sun Tzu, edited by James Clavell, Published by Delacorte Press.

Sincerely,

John "J. R." Moore

CONTENTS

PAGE

... Continued

INTRODUCTION

This book can liberate you! No longer must you or your loved ones have to restrict your lives because of personal security concerns. I have been there and back; my principles are based on first-hand experience from over twenty-five years of street survival.

Learn everything you need to know. What tactics work, and which don't. The training you need and what to avoid. The equipment you need and what you don't need.

Straight talk, nothing held back. Find out what the media isn't telling you. Learn to use this information to your advantage.

You can do it in spite of your age, sex, size or health. Acquire all the information you need to live the productive, full life you and your loved ones deserve.

Share this knowledge, spread it all over. We all need to know how not to be a victim.

Please contact me personally if you have any questions about the suggestions offered in this book.

Good Luck!

Sincerely,

John "J. R." Moore

A NOTE OF CAUTION

This book advocates you consider the possession and use of firearms to defend your life and the lives of those you care about. First however, you must:

1. Find out what your local and state laws are for possession of firearms and carrying of concealed weapons.

2. Find out your local and state laws on self-defense and the use of deadly force in self-defense.

3. Seek an N.R.A. Certified firearms instructor and practice what you learn at least every six months.

This book does not offer legal advice other than to get competent legal advice from your lawyer. There are over 20,000 laws in the U.S.A. for firearms. What is legal and proper in one state may be a crime in another. Before you purchase a firearm or decide to use deadly force to defend your life or that of your family, spend a hundred dollars for an hour with an experienced criminal defense attorney. This doesn't mean a chat with your cousin the cop, or coffee with your buddy, the municipal judge. Spend real money for time with a real lawyer who practices mostly criminal defense law. Get copies of these laws; study them, ask questions. Become your own expert. Inquire about changes at least once a year.

You must find out what the laws are and follow them. If you don't like the laws, then work to change them.

Disregard this advice at your peril. This is not a matter to be taken lightly; COMPLY WITH THE LAW!

Sincerely,

John "J. R." Moore

Chapter 1

THE WORLD AS IT REALLY IS:
Determining what threats exist

"What enables the wise sovereign and the good general to strike and conquer, and achieve things beyond the reach of ordinary men, is foreknowledge."
—The Art of War, by Sun Tzu

*I*t is popular to say that people create their own reality. To a large extent this is true. The "other" reality however, that of "the mean streets," can and will impose itself on you usually when you least expect it. Many adults, especially women living in the city, should plan their activities with personal security concerns in mind. Given the reality of that part of the world over which we have no control; this is prudent.

What is regrettable is that plans get changed, meetings missed, friends not visited and walking across dark areas to parked vehicles become an anguishing task.

Many individuals do not even feel safe in their home. Every summer we read of older folks suffering from heat because of being afraid to open their windows. Home invasion is a growing menace and more likely to happen to you than winning the lottery.

The possibilities for being a target of personal attack are much too numerous for this book to address individually. However, this book will provide a survey of these threats and help you to prepare for coping with them.

The same people the police prepare themselves to deal with, also share your world with you. The level of police preparation has been rising to meet the increased level of threats posed. This has been most apparent to the general public by news coverage of police departments retiring the revolvers they have used since before WWII and issuing high ammunition capacity, 9 mm semi-automatic pistols. This recent trend is already evolving to a change to the more powerful, high ammunition capacity; .45 ACP semi-automatic pistols in California State Patrol; and the FBI with 10 mm pistols.

The reason for this change is the permutations in our society mandating them. Drugs have an impact on our society; and we grow weary of the media attention to this problem. Our concern is twofold:

1. *The crimes perpetrated to acquire funds for the purchase of drugs:* Overwhelming compulsion and drive to fill this need will cause a person to throw reason and caution to the wind. Very often I have someone tell me, "I'll be safe at the *(pick your place)* because there will be a lot of people around. I don't have far to walk, nobody in their right mind would try anything." That's the point; people abusing drugs are not in their right mind.

2. *The mental and physiological changes in a person abusing drugs:* Most people who attended college in the USA between the mid-60s and late- 70s were around casual drug use and may think they know about the subject. Wrong. The lifestyle of criminal drug abuse means getting high for three days at a time. Sleep deprivation without these substances will distort any person's sense of reality. For a person abusing methamphetamine, PCP, alcohol, crack cocaine; or any of the dozens of substances used combined with loss of sleep; creates a person who will bite the toes off his niece or will rape his own mother. This person, who many would regard as dangerous as a large rabid dog, would require the same precautions used to protect innocent life from a rabid dog. A 9 mm semi-automatic will not reliably suffice with one shot with these types; hence the move by police agencies to the more powerful .45 semi-automatic pistols.

As unpleasant as it is to think of such people; they are part of our society. Your chance encounter with one is ultimately what this book will prepare you to deal with.

In most large metropolitan areas it would be rare for more than 10 percent of crimes reported to the police to be reported in the local media. In most areas an excellent solution is to acquire a programmable scanning receiver. These devices are radios that can receive police, fire, state patrol, sheriff, and other public agencies. They cost from one hundred dollars and up and can be programmed to pickup all your local agencies. Your local Radio Shack sells them and the necessary books that list every public agency radio frequency in the United States.

Many people who use scanners are shocked to learn of the volume and type of police calls in their community. Some of the larger police departments such as in the City of St. Louis are using a digital voiceless radio that cannot be monitored with a scanner. In these cases, program your scanner to the paramedics, news agencies and fire department. You will catch the most important events this way.

*****

ACTION ITEMS

1. I will subscribe to and read the largest daily newspaper in my community.

2. I will get a programmable scanning receiver; program it with my local police and fire departments; and listen on a regular basis.

3. I will become familiar with a ten block (one mile) radius area of my home, place of work and any place I frequent.

4. I will become part of my community; meet and talk to my neighbors and local small business owners.

Chapter 2

MENTAL PREPARATION:
Attitude is everything

"The art of war teaches us to rely not on the likelihood of the enemy's not coming, but on our own readiness to receive him, not on the chance of his not attacking; but rather on the fact that we have made our position unassailable."
— <u>The Art of War</u>, by Sun Tzu

*H*aving a positive mental attitude is the key to accomplishing anything. Achieving a sense of feeling safe in personal security matters is no different. Most fears are founded in ignorance or lack of knowledge.

I was once given an assignment to locate a witness who hung-out at an intersection in St. Louis known for its drug sales, shootings and stabbings. It was a cold winter afternoon and my midnight blue Lincoln Town Car sparkled. I wore my brown leather jacket and Ray-ban-shooting sunglasses. I also wore body armor, a 9 mm semi-automatic pistol, and a .38 snubnose revolver.

On my first drive-by of the intersection there were 15-20 people on the corner talking, buying, selling and drinking. I drove by rather slowly trying to pick out my man from the rather cursory description I had been given. When I returned five minutes later, half the crowd was gone. On my third pass the last few people were scampering away.

The following day I stopped down the street three or four car lengths and approached the group on foot. I am white and within minutes was conversing with 5 or 6 black men from the corner. They looked me over and quickly decided that I was armed. I was later told by one whom I hired to lead me to my witness; that the day before the assembled group was convinced that the window of my Lincoln was going to have a sub-machine gun thrust out and fired at them.

The police routinely patrol these parts of St. Louis with two patrol cars, one on the bumper of the other. I went in alone with no back-up, found what I came for and left with no harm to me.

I once knew a police woman as gutsy as any man I've met. She worked the streets of a small high-crime municipality next to St. Louis at night. She was just over five feet tall and not much more than a hundred pounds. I questioned her on her ability to subdue male suspects alone. She revealed a can-do attitude that left no room for failure. From the bottom of her well-worn combat boots to her curly hair, she was prepared daily to take on anything the streets had to offer.

Those of us who live and survive on the "mean streets" have more than training and equipment. We have a positive mental attitude (PMA). If you aren't familiar with the concept, the classic book on the subject is <u>Success Through a Positive Mental Attitude</u> by Napoleon Hill and W. Clement Stone. The bottom line is: if you don't have a positive mental attitude ... *get one.*

You will find that your PMA is an evolving matter. As you study, learn new skills and acquire equipment your PMA will grow. It will be a gradual upward march from whatever beginning point you start from; to where you "feel safe anywhere." Given a reasonable level of persistence and resources, you can and will get there. It will be fun if you decide it to be so. It will be spiritually invigorating if you let it become that. You are the one in charge of your life and learning these skills will only liberate you to be all that you choose to be.

*****

ACTION ITEMS

1. I will immediately start to improve my mental attitude.

2. I will accomplish this by:

a. Finding out what a Positive Mental Attitude is.

b. Getting the necessary training and skills I need to "Feel Safe Anywhere." (More specifics in later chapters)

c. Practicing the above until I really feel my entire being is totally prepared for anything that happens.

Chapter 3

DEADLY FORCE:
When you can use it

"The skillful tactician may be likened to the Shuai-Jan. Now the Shuai-Jan is a snake that is found in the Ch'ang mountains. Strike at its head, and you will be attacked by its tail; strike at its tail, and you will be attacked by its head; strike at its middle, and you will be attacked by head and tail both."
                                    —The Art of War, by Sun Tzu

*F*irst, a definition of what is generally considered to be deadly force is in order. Most prosecuting attorneys regard a weapon such as a gun or knife to be an instrument capable of delivering deadly force. While tear-gas would not be considered deadly force, an instrument such as a baseball bat falls in a gray area. Using a weapon or instrument that is capable of causing death against a person is considered to be the use of deadly force.

In many states, a person must (as long as it is reasonable) retreat from the threat of deadly force, before he or she may lawfully meet that threat with deadly force. How, when, or if you retreat, are rather subjective matters. You are not, for example, expected to jump from a second floor window before you defend yourself with deadly force. You are not expected to abandon your home either.

What you need to remember is:

1. Retreat from the attack as long as it is reasonable.
2. Only use deadly force to meet deadly force.

If you have more questions on this matter *consult an attorney who handles criminal defense work.*

For most people a firearm first comes to mind when they think of deadly force. If you use a firearm you have to get it right the first time.

I have on several occasions used firearms while defending my home. I have yet to discharge a weapon while using it to defend my home. On one occasion, I was sitting in the bathtub when I heard a noise at the bathroom window. I got dressed (neglecting to put on shoes) armed myself with a Colt 9 mm Combat Commander and instructed my wife to call the police before I slipped out the back door.

When I opened the back door, I saw a young man standing on a steel barrel at my bathroom window. He immediately ran, with me in pursuit. I chased him two blocks barefoot past a city maintenance building where a man was standing in an open door. I must have been quite a sight running barefoot, shirt tails flying, pistol in-hand and chasing a man down the street. I called out for him to call the police as I ran past. I lost the young man at the end of the block and was limping home when the police cruiser came speeding up to me. I confirmed that I was the man chasing the other down the street. I was told to put my gun away and go home, so I did.

One week later, I again heard a noise from the bathroom window. This time I made sure to put on shoes. *(I broke a toe the previous week)* I went quietly out the front door this time. As I came around the corner of the building, I caught a glimpse of movement, looked up and saw the same young man on the roof of my building hanging onto the gutter and attempting to peer into my bathroom. I pointed my pistol at him and ordered him not to move. He ran to the opposite side of the roof. I ran to the same side and repeated my order. He ran to still another side of the roof. I ran to that side and told him I would shoot him if he ran again. He didn't run.

When the police arrived three minutes later, I had the young man off the roof and leaning against the building with his hands and feet spread. The police spent several hours trying to locate an adult where he lived. They also repeatedly told him how fortunate he was to have been captured by me rather than shot by some hothead.

In both cases cited above I used implements of deadly force. In the first case I would have definitely been in the wrong to fire at the suspect. The second case was more of a gray area. It was very dark and the young man who was 5 foot 8 inches tall and looked like an adult from my view. My concern while confronting him was that he would have a gun. If he had made a move that looked like he was going to draw a weapon, I would have had to decide in seconds what to do next.

I had already made up my mind. If a weapon had appeared, he was going down. Sound drastic? Does this upset you? In a situation as just discussed, life gets down to very basic levels quickly. You stop the bad guy before that person gets you, period. No time for intellectual debate; no time to consider the abused childhood of the bad guy. It's you or the other person.

No second chance. No prize for second place. Hesitate and you may be dead. Act irrationally and you wound or kill an unarmed person. This is as serious as it gets. You must be absolutely certain the first time and stick by that decision.

Get good training. Practice what you learn. Get so good that you can make that split second decision with confidence.

DEADLY FORCE: AFTER YOU HAVE USED IT
It's over. Although it only lasted less than ten minutes, you have used a firearm to defend your family against a home invasion.

There is a dead guy lying at the foot of your stairway; your heart is pounding; your wife has called the police; and your mind is trying to digest the events of the last few minutes. Then, the first police cruiser pulls up in front of your home.

So what to do?

First, unload your firearm, and lay it down in plain sight.

Second, get dressed.

Third, call your lawyer.

Fourth, start a pot of coffee, it's going to be a long night.

What you do next depends on a number of factors. Depending on who you are and the facts of the situation, *most attorneys will tell you not give a statement to the police until your attorney is present.* Do what your lawyer tells you to do. Don't listen to anyone else.

At a minimum give the police your full name, date of birth and place of residence. Provide them with your driver's license or other identification. Inform them that your lawyer has told you not to give a statement until he is present. Be as polite and business like as possible. Most police officers are trained to both expect and respect your desire to *wait until your attorney is present before giving a statement.* Even if they don't allow time for your attorney to come, it is your choice and right, don't give it up.

Do you know the dead person? If you do, *it would probably be advisable not to speak to the police unless your attorney is present.* I have personally seen people charged with homicide while defending their lives; only to have the charges dropped or reduced to manslaughter after a lengthy, expensive investigation and defense effort by an experienced criminal defense attorney and criminal defense investigator.

If on the other hand, your home was invaded by a total stranger who was armed with a deadly weapon, who you had reason to believe meant harm to you and your family, your firearm and your ownership of it conforms to all existing state and local laws, you are stone cold sober, and a model citizen in your community; then you can give a statement to the police, *with your lawyer's consent.*

The possible scenarios are limited only to your imagination regarding how you may have to defend yourself. The only all inclusive answer is to *give a statement to the police only with your attorney present.* While this may be inconvenient, the several hours delay while waiting could avoid months of aggravation and thousands of dollars in expenses.

*****

ACTION ITEMS

1. I will find out and memorize what is considered deadly force and when I can use it where I live:

a. The use of deadly force in my community is ...

_____

_____

_____

b. I can use deadly force in my community by ...

_____

_____

_____

2. I will practice my skills of self-defense until I feel confident in my ability to react with the appropriate force.

3. If I use deadly force, *I will give a statement to the police only with my attorney present.*

Chapter 4

YOUR HOME IS YOUR CASTLE

"When you surround an army, leave an outlet free. This does not mean that the enemy is to be allowed to escape. The object is to make him believe that there is a road to safety, and thus prevent his fighting with the courage of despair."
— <u>The Art of War</u>, by Sun Tzu

*T*he one place where you control the environment is your home; and where all sights, sounds and smells are familiar. Having a safe and secure home is essential for a happy life. The objective here is to provide some ideas on creating the desired level of security without creating a feeling of being "locked in." First comes the location of your home. What are the perceived threats in your neighborhood? For example, if home invasions have been occurring in your area, you may opt for good quality deadbolt locks on your exterior doors; and perhaps upgrade existing doors to steel doors and frames. The good quality ones are very attractive.

LIGHTING (exterior)

Effective exterior lighting is a basic part of home security. While 360° of lighting around the home is most desirable, be sure to light, at minimum, the front and back door areas. Your security lighting does not have to be harsh institutional bright. Go for a more attractive, decorative look. If you live in an apartment or condominium, work with the landlord or condo management group to ensure that lighting is adequate. *The rule here is: Lights on outside, all night, every night.*

LIGHTING (interior)

The objective here is to provide a "lived in, people at home" look. Be consistent, use your self-timers all the time; not just when you're away. There should be some lights on all night every night. Use night lights in the bathrooms, perhaps one in the kitchen too. Little glowing plug-in switchless night lights are very handy in bedrooms and hallways. *The rule here is: Make it appear that people are at home, all night, every night.*

ALARMS

To a greater extent, the benefits of an alarm system are being recognized. The highest level of security here is provided by a monitored system. A monitored system is one that connects your home alarm to a central security office manned 24 hours 7 days a week. When your alarm activates, it instantly notifies the security office who in turn contact the appropriate agency such as, police, fire and paramedics. Some of the larger alarm companies respond with their own people. If an alarm system is your decision, be sure to price shop; prices can vary by hundreds of dollars for essentially the same service. The nationwide companies, such as Brinks, offer tremendous value in their basic service package, and is a good baseline for price comparison. Try to have a clear idea of what you want before contacting an alarm company. They are in business to sell their services and may sell you more than you need. For most people I suggest only the basic package with a panic button feature in the master bedroom and "safe" room. *(More on this later)*

Be certain to have a siren or loud horn connected to your alarm, especially for your "panic button." If it costs extra, don't hesitate to pay it.

There are two basic tactics to alarm systems. The *first* is to have a silent alarm where there is no warning at the home, only an alarm at the central office. The *second* is for a siren and possibly lights to go on at the home, as well as the alarm at the central office. You will want the second. *You want as much noise and lights going on as possible when a bad guy is in your home.*

INSURANCE
Adequate insurance is part of the picture. Homeowner's or renter's insurance policies are a necessity. Be sure you have it and that you have a current inventory of all valuables on file with your agent; along with any necessary riders to cover them. Photographs, appraisals and current video tape recordings of these valuables will end arguments about claims. A little known bonus to the above policies is that they may cover valuables stolen from your vehicle or while on vacation. *Keep insurance photos and videos in a safe deposit box.*

DOORS, WINDOWS, LOCKS
Find a professional locksmith. For the most part, in the overall industry, they tend to be some of the most down-to-earth people I've met. If you feel you have special needs, seek the advice of a professional. If you are the first occupant of your home or apartment, get your locks re-keyed now. For the sake of convenience get them "keyed alike" where one key works all locks. All exterior doors should have at least one deadbolt along with the entrance lock. If you have windows in your

doors or in arm's reach, the deadbolt should be either out of arm's reach (allow for long arms) or of the double cylinder type. These require a key on the inside. Don't develop the bad habit of leaving a key in the inside cylinder; attach it on a hanger well away from the door. *Attach reflective tape (automotive type) to the hanger. For fire safety, be positive everyone knows its location.*

Doors are a vulnerable area for entrance. A solid-core wood door with three heavy hinges, an entrance lock and deadbolt lock will discourage most bad guys. If your area requires upgrades, go to a complete steel door and frame. If you are a renter, work with your landlord on having the cost deducted from your rent. A professional installation adds to the value of the property. Garage doors are often little more than thin plastic, and patio-doors are well known for their vulnerability. Here is where your alarm company can install switches and detectors much more cost effectively than you can upgrade these doors.

Windows are quite vulnerable. If your neighbors have bars on their windows and you don't, you make yourself a target. The reports of tragedies, because of people being unable to escape a burning home because of security bars, is a very real concern. If you live in an area where having security bars on your windows is necessary, consider having them installed inside the home. If the security bar sales and installation company you contact cannot provide inside bars that a child can open, then find one that can. Check with your local fire department or building inspector. The installation of window and door security bars is being regulated by more local governments throughout the country.

Your locksmith can upgrade the locks on any type of window to the point where gaining entrance will mean virtually destroying the window. This means noise and time, both of which the bad guys dislike.

DOGS

Bad guys don't like dogs. Their hearing and smell are several times more acute than humans and they bark when alerted. Homes that have a dog inside are very difficult to invade without the dog being alerted. Women that have inside dogs will seldom wake up to a stranger in their bedroom. There are two basic concepts to follow when owning a dog for personal security:

1. Own a small dog that will bark when alerted to danger.

2. Own a large dog that will alert you to danger and attack the bad guy on your command.

By far the first is the most popular choice for the majority of people. It presents the most options in picking a breed and requires minimal training. The second choice gets serious and expensive very quickly. An outside dog is, with rare exceptions, somewhat easily compromised by poisoned meat. *An inside dog will always be on alert for your protection.*

CHOOSING A DOG

For the first category, most small breeds commonly known to be good house dogs are adequate. For the second, I recommend only the Timber Shepherd®, bred and sold by LRRP K-9 Services, Box 1620 ME, Aiken, South Carolina 29802, 803-649-5936. I don't need to promote these people, contact them and they will sell themselves to you.

CAUTION ON ATTACK DOGS

Your insurance agent will either charge you a higher premium or cancel you. Even the finest and best trained dogs have been known to injure a child or visitor. Be advised, these are powerful animals, always keep this foremost in any decision you make.

TRAINING YOUR DOG

The training of a small house dog will be minimal beyond being housebroken. For an attack dog however, be prepared to invest considerable time learning to properly train the dog to your commands. The better breeders (like LRRP K-9 Services) can provide in-house assistance in training. Any reputable breeder will give you references to a good training facility.

SAFE ROOM

The concept is to take one room of your home and make it a safe haven. *A room with a reinforced door, a strong lock, a telephone, and if you desire, a weapon to defend yourself with.* Most often the safe room will be a bedroom or bathroom. In his book <u>To Ride, Shoot Straight, and Speak the Truth</u>, Jeff Cooper advocates the installation of an iron gate across the hallway separating the bedrooms from the rest of the home. With this you can stop the intruder and shoot through the gate if necessary.

TELEPHONE SERVICE

Contact your telephone company about having your entrance cable installed underground. Have the entrance cable installed in metal conduit if an underground installation is not feasible. Another option is to bring your cellular phone inside, and keep it on a charger in your safe room. An unlisted telephone may stop obscene calls, but it won't stop telephone solicitors or computer calls. If call screening is available in your area, get it; if it is not, get a telephone answering machine. Screen your calls when you are home and just push a button to record threatening calls.

I won't allow a cordless telephone in my house. The reason for this is that, *anyone with one hundred dollars and the desire, can listen to every word on your cordless telephone.* The frequencies used are published by Radio Shack and they also sell the necessary radios to intercept the telephone calls.

ELECTRIC SERVICE
Here you also can get your electric service installed underground.

GARAGE DOOR OPENERS
Not only can you open your door but also turn on as many lights as you choose, from the comfort of the driver's seat.

NEIGHBORHOOD WATCH GROUPS
In the days before TV and air-conditioning, evenings were spent on front porches and neighbors talked to each other. We now attempt to intentionally structure and replace at least a portion of what has been lost through these watch groups. They can and do work. If your street does not have one, start one. Most police departments will lend assistance to your group by providing the necessary training and guidelines. Getting to meet your neighbors may even be fun.

If you live far enough out in the country, neighbors still take care of each other and to a large extent you are your own police force. The response time from the sheriff's department may be 45 minutes or more in some areas.

*****

ACTION ITEMS

1. Neighborhood and Building Watch Groups

Watch Group leader's name and telephone:

_____

_____

My neighbors' names and telephones:

_____

_____

_____

_____

_____

2. My Outside Lighting

Street: _____adequate _____call city

Front Door: _____adequate _____install_____ repair

Entranceways: _____adequate _____install_____ repair

Stairs: _____adequate _____install_____ repair

Halls:_____adequate _____install_____ repair

Back Door: _____adequate _____install_____ repair

3. My Entrance Doors: Front and Rear

☐ Solid-core wood or steel door and frame

☐ Have peephole

☐ Doors inadequate: repair or replace by _____

4. My House Locks

☐ Deadbolt Front & Rear

☐ Inadequate: replace or upgrade by _____

5. My Window Locks

☐ Prevent entry unless frame is destroyed

☐ Inadequate: must upgrade by _____

6. My Window Treatment

☐ Prevents unauthorized view of interior

☐ Must be upgraded by_____

7. Dogs

☐ I am considering the acquisition of a dog

☐ If I get a dog, it will be the right one for me and I'll get proper training for it and knowledge for myself.

8. My Alarm System

☐ Is professional, monitored

☐ Has a panic button

☐ I must upgrade with _____, and upgrade by _____

9. My Telephone Service Entry Cable

☐ Is underground

☐ Is shielded in metal conduit

☐ Is exposed and must be upgraded by _____

☐ I will get caller ID or an answering machine by_____, and use it.

☐ If I have a cordless telephone, I will restrict its use.

10. My Electric Service

☐ Is underground

☐ Is shielded in metal conduit

☐ Is exposed and must be upgraded by_____

11. My Interior Lights

☐ Are adequate and on timers

☐ Must be upgraded with _____
by _____

12. My Defensive Firearm

☐ Is clean, loaded, accessible to me

☐ Is secure from unauthorized use

☐ I will get a defensive firearm by _____ and
start training _____

13. My Home Insurance

☐ Is in force and covers everything I own

☐ I have current inventory and appraisals on file with my
agent.

☐ Must be purchased or upgraded by _____

14. My Safe Room

☐ Is complete and ready for use

☐ Is still being worked on and requires the following:

_____

_____

Chapter 5

YOUR AUTOMOBILE AS A DEFENSIVE INSTRUMENT

"Place your army in deadly peril, and it will survive; plunge it into desperate straits, and it will come through in safety."
—The Art of War, by Sun Tzu

*F*or most Americans their automobile is their main means of transportation. Selection is usually based on a number of criteria. Unfortunately, personal security is rarely one. Following is a discussion of selection based on personal security.

In many places you can increase your personal security by buying a car that looks like an unmarked police car. In this case, a current Chevrolet Caprice four door in a plain color, with black wall tires, a chrome spotlight on the driver's side, and several discreet professional looking antennas will accomplish this. The downside to this tactic is that in some neighborhoods you may be attacked, shot at and harassed if the punks on the street think you are a cop.

I generally recommend full-size American sedans with V-8 engines, automatic transmissions and full power. Why the full power? Because the driver can control all the windows and locks nearly instantly without moving. Why an automatic transmission? Because you can drive and shoot at the same time if necessary. I know this is advice that will be attacked as imprudent or ill-advised by some police officials. They, however, have no responsibility to protect you or your loved ones as individuals, only the community at large.

The Chevrolet Suburban with a big V-8 presents a formidable presence on the street. Other good examples are the Jeep Cherokee, Ford Explorer, Dodge Ram Wagon. Get the idea? Size and power are what's important, full-size vans are great also. Recommended options: Largest V-8 offered, Trailoring package; these usually include heavy-duty transmissions, low-gear rear-ends, transmission coolers and heavy-duty springs. Get the limited slip rear-end and with proper tires you'll go in most snow or ice conditions. Four wheel drive is of marginal help unless you live in a rural area or far enough north to get more snow. Power everything for reasons previously mentioned.

TIRES
Michelin all-weather steel-belted radials; anything less and you're fooling yourself. Get the lowest, widest tires that will fit your wheels without rubbing the car.

ALARMS
They really do work. The ones that sound when you walk past can be a nuisance. Consider one that allows you to start your car remotely or even more important, one that allows you to activate the siren remotely. An often overlooked feature is the ability to start the siren and lights with an override switch from inside the vehicle.

DRIVING

Few drivers ever push the limits of their car or driving ability absent a compelling reason.

The Sports Car Club of America (SCCA) sanctions a competition called Solo racing. Here each car runs alone, or solo, on a course consisting of rubber traffic cones on a large parking lot against the clock. There is a class for every type of vehicle from race cars to pickup trucks. It's great fun and you'll learn to increase your limits and the limits of your vehicle. Once you meet these people you can easily go "all the way" as far as driving skills are concerned.

When driving on the street be aware of 360° around your car, get a couple of convex mirrors that attach to your outside rear view mirrors (small one on the driver's side, larger one on the passenger side) and learn to use them. Never get so close to a car in front of you at an intersection, that you can't go around without backing first.

In a bad area stay in the extreme left lane so you have an escape route and are farther from the curb, keep your pistol under your thigh ready for instant use.

Being attacked while in your vehicle (carjacking) is becoming more common on the east and west coasts. The growing popularity of car alarms makes theft of occupied vehicles more attractive. My solution is to fight back. If an armed thug attacks you and you cannot drive away, start your alarm siren to scare off the attacker. If you cannot drive the person away and he or she persists in the attack, shoot. Here again is where liberals and some police officials will want you to be a passive victim while your family is being attacked. Don't fall for it. They won't be there for you in your time of need. Their progressive thoughts about crime and criminals won't protect you, but a loaded .45 automatic will.

Being "bumped" from behind is a popular way to get you out of your vehicle. Don't fall for it. Roll down your window far enough to talk, and agree to have the other car follow you to an open service station. Get the other car's license plate number before starting away. Try to remember descriptions (race, sex, age, height, weight, hair, clothing) and write them down.

You're driving home one night, you're female, alone and believe that you are being followed ...

... Don't go home. This will only make a serious problem worse.

... To verify if you are being followed; on a four lane street, drive 10 MPH below the speed limit for two blocks, most people will pass you. On a two-lane or to become more positive, drive around a block, and return to your original route.

... Once you know you are being followed, drive to the nearest police or fire station; now is the time to learn where they are in your area. Get to and use the most heavily traveled streets. If the police and fire station locations are unknown, or too far, go to the nearest all night convenience store, service station; get inside and call the police.

... If you are about to be attacked, park close to the front door of a store, lock your car doors, honk your horn, flash your headlights. If the attack persists, shoot the attacker.

CELLULAR TELEPHONES

These handy little devices can be lifesavers. The best ones for personal security are also inexpensive. The transportable "bag-phone" is a totally self-contained, full-power unit you can carry and use anywhere you are in range of a cell tower. Get one.

STORM KIT

The contents will depend on where you are and the time of year. The basics include: Three day supply of food and water, candles, flashlight (spare bulbs & batteries) blanket, sturdy walking shoes, First aid kit, one hundred dollars in twenties, and a backpack to carry it all in.

ANTI-THEFT DEVICES

Those steering wheel locks that are bright red will deter most amateurs from trying to steal your car. Some expensive car stereos now have removable face-plates. The rule here is to cover-up, conceal or remove from sight anything that can be stolen and sold. Radar detectors, expensive sunglasses, leather jackets, anything of value.

HOW & WHY TO REGISTER YOUR VEHICLE

Many people don't know it, but the registration of your automobile license plate is public record. Anyone can obtain the name and address of record for your license plate. Change your registration. This strategy is one I use in training rookie investigators. Those that fail to do so have had unexpected, potentially dangerous incidents where individuals have located an investigator's residence through motor vehicle registration.

1. Register your vehicle to an address where you don't live.

   a. Be creative. Use your lawyer's office (with permission) or rent one of those boxes at a private mailbox business and you will have a street and suite address.

For even greater security,

1. Register a fictitious name (such as Blue Knight Investigations) with your secretary of state,

2. Register your vehicle to the fictitious name. Be sure your insurance company and loan company approve your plan.

MAINTENANCE OF YOUR VEHICLE
If your car won't start and run properly, all the advice mentioned above will very quickly become "none of the above."

1. Follow the maintenance schedule in your owner's manual.

2. Keep a properly inflated spare tire and learn how to change it.

3. Never have under a half-tank of fuel in your vehicle.

4. Get the largest, most powerful battery that will fit in your car. At this writing the Sears Die Hard Gold is it. KEEP THE TERMINALS CLEAN & TIGHT! Dirty terminals are the single most common reason for a car not starting.

5. Now that you're driving on Michelins, make sure they are replaced before they wear out.

6. Before you drive, do a walk around. Check your tires for proper inflation. Check all lights and windows for cleanliness.

Make sure your mirrors are adjusted and check all your gauges once the engine is running.

7. Assuming you change your oil every 2,500 miles *(and you should)* check your belts and hoses at the same time.

*****

ACTION ITEMS

1. I will modify my current automobile or acquire one more suited for my defensive needs by _____

2. I will only use Michelins or similar high-quality steel-belted radials from now on

3. I will equip my vehicle with an alarm by _____

4. I will learn my driving limits and improve my driving skills

5. I will memorize my plan of actions for street scenarios

6. I will get a cellular telephone by _____

7. I will prepare a storm kit for my car by _____

8. I will make my car more theft resistant

9. I will register my vehicle away from my residence by _____

10. I will properly maintain my car:

    Last maintenance _____

    Next maintenance by _____

Chapter 6

THE MEAN STREETS

"Earth comprises distances, great and small; danger and security; open ground and narrow passes; the chances of life and death."

—The Art of War, by Sun Tzu

You are walking down a dark empty street by yourself. Virtually no street in any metropolitan area of the United States is more than a few minutes drive from places inhabited by evil people. You're on your own out there. Just you and what you bring with you. Here are some tips:

1. When you leave home, leave your personal stereo at home. You need all your senses, blocking out your sense of hearing only gives the bad guys an advantage.

2. Wear shoes and clothing that will allow you to run.

3. Arm yourself. I've worked with a client whose wife went jogging one day carrying only a garage door opener. Her body

was found nearly two years later. She died alone, in terror of her captor. Get a pistol, learn how to shoot, and carry it.

I was out for a walk on a dark evening a couple of years ago. I was in another city, staying at a downtown motel. I soon found, on my route to see the river, I was walking down a street that had no people, no cars, only closed warehouses. I also noticed that I was walking down the middle of the street. I hadn't consciously decided to do so. It is a habit I learned while patrolling alleys at night in Vietnam by myself. *The point here is to develop habits that will keep you alive.*

So how does one go about acquiring *street smarts?* You first learn basic skills of martial arts and firearms handling. You then become a student of people. Learn to watch, really look at people, not past them. Think about what you see. Are they watching and looking. Most people don't do these things. Do they exhibit unusual behavior like ... paying extra attention to the contents of parked cars, turning away when a police cruiser goes past. Are they wearing cold weather clothing when it's above 70°? Are they looking at you?

There will often be various scenarios shown in local news coverage of crimes. Read and watch for these, they will give you insight on what is being done to people in your area.

My wife and I left a symphony concert one-half hour early and found ourselves walking alone down the street at about 9:30 p.m. As we went past a group of men on a corner, one young man (mid-twenties six-foot plus and muscular) called out to us asking if we had change for a twenty. My hand tightened around the butt of my .38 Smith & Wesson in my pocket as my wife and I said "NO" loudly in unison and kept walking. The point here is threefold:

First: Avoid any confrontation such as this possible "set up."

Second: Keep moving. They have to get you stopped before they can attack you.

Third: Make sure you're armed.

One sunny afternoon, I was on the street about to get in my car when a man approached me and asked for bus fare. My hand was holding the Smith & Wesson in my pocket as he quickly and rather convincingly added that he meant me no harm. I gave him a dollar. People can tell when you have no fear, that you are in control.

WALKING
Learn to think about and use your senses of hearing, sight, smell and touch on the street. Be alert to what is going on not just in your immediate vicinity, but down the street in both directions. Avoid possible ambush sites such as alleyways, abandoned buildings, weed covered lots and corners frequented by bad guys. If a strange car slows down next to you, be prepared to run in the opposite direction of the car.

Learn to walk erect, with your head up; take long purposeful steps, swing your arms naturally. Look from side to side. If you believe someone is following you, cross the street. If you're sure someone is following you, seek the nearest safe haven such as an occupied home or open place of business.

If you are about to be attacked, run if you believe you can get away. If not, seek a defensive position, place a parked car between you and the attacker, *(I've done this)* run around the car yelling for help and plan your next move. In my case, I frustrated my attacker for several minutes until the police arrived and arrested the attacker.

PUBLIC TRANSPORTATION

Those who use public transportation have their unique situations. There are long waits at usually dark isolated places and little or no police protection on the conveyance. Men and women traveling alone on public transportation are often chosen to be victims. Don't be a victim! You have every right to defend yourself! The decision to arm yourself however must be balanced against your local laws. More and more people have decided they will do what the police cannot do; protect themselves.

On a bus, sit near the front. If you have a bag or case and the bus is nearly empty, place it on the seat next to you. This will make it more difficult for an unwanted companion to sit next to you. If you believe someone is going to get off at your stop to attack you, don't get off. Remain on the bus until you can get off right in front of an open business, or tell the driver your concern and ask for his/her help.

Commuter trains sometimes are the worst place for civil people. They have lonely underground stations and cars with no police. Very often you are really on your own. The highly publicized case of Bernard Goetz in the New York City subway defending himself with a pistol against several armed attackers shows how crazy the world is when the victim becomes the criminal. Demand your right to carry a firearm!

Do whatever you must to get a permit to carry a concealed weapon. The liberal fools *(personal opinion)* that run New York City wanted Mr. Goetz in jail to serve as an example to anyone else foolish enough to believe they should defend their life with a firearm.

HOTELS, MOTELS

When I go to sleep in a motel room I have on the nightstand next to the bed a .38, flashlight and a pair of trousers nearby. If there is a knock at my door and I'm not expecting someone, I answer with my pistol in my hand. Lock the chain before going to sleep, it will make enough noise to wake you when it breaks. When possible, park your car where you can see it from your window. Unless the car has an alarm system, bring inside everything of value from it. Ground level rooms near exits are the most likely to be hit by the bad guys, but there is no guaranty of security in other areas.

INNER CITY LIFE IN THE USA

Most middle-class citizens never venture into the inner city except to take a short-cut. Here are some observations:

Hardened stores: These are convenience stores, liquor stores, carry-out restaurants. You walk in to the front door, walk six or eight feet, and can go no farther. You stop at a counter that runs the width of the store. From the top of the counter to the ceiling is bullet-resistant Lexan. There is a sliding drawer large enough for a bag of groceries. You tell the clerk which items you wish to buy; the clerk retrieves them and totals up the sale. You then put your money in the drawer, the clerk places your purchases and change in the drawer, and slides the drawer back to you.

The shooting starts at sunset: I was working with another investigator in the ghetto. He is a black Vietnam Veteran and very street-wise. We were preparing for a night surveillance when he told me "John, the shooting starts at sunset." We got our bullet resistant vests on and assumed our positions in the public housing project. About one-tenth of the apartments in the two- story complex had plywood covering the window openings. There was much foot traffic, particularly near where the drugs were being sold. Shortly after sunset I radioed my partner that I heard small-arms fire. He responded like-wise. A few minutes later I reported hearing a short burst of automatic weapons fire. My partner wasn't surprised. The city police after cruising past me to run my license plate, stopped to chat. They were running two cruisers, one on the bumper of the other. I was considered suspicious because I was white in a black neighborhood. The officers' curiosity, what a white man would be doing in this area after dark, had to be satisfied.

Other than friends shot in Vietnam, I, as most middle-class whites, don't personally know a single person who has been shot. It's different in the ghetto. Virtually everyone has a personal acquaintance who has been knifed, shot or murdered; perhaps even several acquaintances.

Random nightly gunfire is the rule, not the exception. The dope-crazed people who have reduced life in the inner-city to what it has become are only a few minutes drive in a stolen car from where you live, work and shop.

One morning I was in a US Post Office, conducting business through a one and one-half inch thick piece of Lexan. All new schools are built with very few ground level windows. The ground level windows they do have are six-inch wide slits. The school children have laminated ID badges so the armed guards can tell them from the trespassers. At the high schools the regular police arrive at the end of the school day to prevent fights between rival gangs.

The point here is that the bad guys have reduced life to what it is in the inner-city; and have more mobility. The likelihood of your chance encounter with one of them is greater today than ever before due to their increasing numbers.

*****

ACTION ITEMS

1. I will prepare myself physically and mentally to prevail on the mean streets.

2. I will become observant and aware of my surroundings.

3. I will find out the proper and legal way to carry a concealed weapon where I live, and do it.

4. I will make sensible precautions part of my daily routine.

Chapter 7

MARTIAL ARTS:
What you do and don't need

"He who exercises no forethought but makes light of his opponents is sure to be captured by them."
— The Art of War, by Sun Tzu

Very few adult women and most men have no recent experience of being bodily picked up and thrown to the ground. Men who have participated in contact sports have had the experience of being violently knocked around and have learned to respond appropriately. Those men who have not played contact sports and virtually all women are at a distinct disadvantage in a violent confrontation.

For most adults, being struck with a fist, grabbed or tackled is so totally foreign to their experience that they become disoriented and virtually paralyzed and react with no response. The bad guys know you will probably respond this way and depend on it to get their attack on you off to a good start. Imagine how surprised the bad guy would be to have his or her initial blow deflected by your forearm as you draw a pistol with your free hand. This is how it should be. This is how you can and will respond if you decide to train yourself, equip yourself and maintain your skill level through regular practice.

Martial arts training should accomplish two basic goals:

1. Expose you to violent physical contact; get knocked around a bit and bounce back in a proper manner.

2. Teach you to break holds, deliver painful blows and escape.

I do not advocate becoming an advanced student of any given martial arts discipline. Rather, I believe you should seek out an instructor who will provide the same training in martial arts that is given to police cadets. That is to learn a few, but very effective moves, that will accomplish the goals listed above. The only equipment you should need would be a sweat-suit. Dressing in a medieval oriental farmer's outfit or becoming proficient with chrome-plated replicas of medieval oriental farm tools, probably will not satisfy your needs. This advanced training will make you well qualified to engage a medieval oriental farmer in combat, but not in what you need to protect yourself. Just learn to stick to the basics.

So where do you go? Ask the training officer of your local police department who they use. If you approach the owner of a martial arts school, be very clear and firm as to the nature of your inquiry or you may soon find yourself wearing a rice farmer's suit, bowing to your instructor and learning all kinds of oriental techniques in the martial arts. You may be told how "necessary" these advanced techniques are for your protection. Your response should be "I want to learn what a police cadet learns, period."

My advise relates to this book's audience and what the average person will find useful to incorporate into his or her daily life.

In fairness to serious students of the martial arts there is much value in long term study. The benefits are numerous. Students develop mental and physical discipline, physical fitness, spiritual peace and self-confidence. If advanced study in martial arts appears worthwhile to you, go for it!

Your local community college, YMCA or YWCA may offer courses in self-defense. Check them out.

*****

ACTION ITEMS

1. I will get training in basic, no frills, unarmed self-defense techniques by _____

2. I will avoid oriental techniques and learn only what I need

3. I will practice what I learn often enough to remain proficient.

Chapter 8

FIREARMS:
Proper role, use, selection and training

"The art of war is of vital importance to the state. It is a matter of life and death, a road to safety or ruin. Hence, under no circumstances can it be neglected."
　　　　　　　　　　　　　　　—The Art of War, by Sun Tzu

*I*n any book of this nature, the parts dealing with the use of firearms are the most controversial. Any person who is considering arming themselves in America in the 1990s is faced with a number of decisions and questions. My liberal friends are deeply offended by the thought that a person feels the need to defend their life with a firearm. At the same time they offer no viable alternative as to how a people are to defend their lives against armed assailants. Their world is one of fantasy where they cling to their ideal of a weapon-free crime-free society and their hope to achieve this goal.

The streets the rest of us live on, however, are ones which increasingly bring random violent crime to innocent people.

Since the late 1960s our "enlightened" mental health profes-
sionals have made long-term hospitalization of the mentally
ill a thing of the past. The murderer Lori Dann and would-be
assassin John Hinckley are well-known examples of people
with histories of mental illness when they committed their
crimes.

Men with long arrest records and multiple convictions are
placed on probation, only to commit more crimes.

I like to tell my liberal friends that when the county government is ready to post a performance bond guaranteeing the
performance of the police department in protecting my family, I will gladly give up my firearms. There is, of course, no
response because no police department owes you a personal
obligation to protect you or your loved ones. If they fail to
protect you, you have no recourse, because there was no
obligation there to begin with.

If you believe that a key protruding between your fingers or
a whistle or tear-gas will stop a 250 pound man high on crack,
bent on doing you harm, consider this: Your non-lethal
weapon might stop the attack, but you're stacking the odds
against yourself.

The only positive method of stopping a determined, dangerous attacker is with a firearm.

PISTOLS
A pistol is a reactive tool, you carry it when you might need
it. The best pistol for self-defense is the .45 ACP automatic.
It is powerful enough to knockdown the biggest man, even if
he is wearing body-armor. With proper training even a small
person can learn to be competent with one. The Colt® Government .45 ACP still sets the standard by which all others
are measured. The big .45 however may require more training

than many are willing to devote, or they may find even the smallest version of the .45 too large and heavy to conceal or carry on a daily basis.

When a compact, light-weight, relatively inexpensive, pistol of acceptable power requiring a minimal amount of training is called for I usually recommend the .38 special Smith & Wesson Model 38 bodyguard. It is very compact, only $6\frac{5}{16}$" long and weighs 14 ounces. It holds five rounds of .38 Special ammunition; a round used by major police departments with varying levels of success. I say varying because of the numerous times when a large man high on drugs has taken multiple hits in the chest only to continue his attack.

As much as I like the big automatics, I acknowledge that many people don't and won't take the time necessary to learn how to use them. This is why the Model 38 is so good. There is no safety, no cocking; nothing to do except to aim and squeeze the trigger.

If you have a social occasion where even the Model 38 is too large, a compact pistol is the North American Mini-Revolver. It is a 5-shot .22 revolver that is $3\frac{5}{8}$" long and weighs four ounces.

Pistols are best used when away from home. Carrying a concealed weapon is not a matter to be taken lightly. The laws vary from state to state and I often meet criminal defense attorneys that do not know some of the more obscure points of these laws. The police, even chiefs of police, do not always know these fine points, or will withhold information from you if they don't like citizens to be armed. The National Rifle Association maintains up-to-date copies of all state statutes on firearms. As a member you have access to their services. The membership telephone number is 1-800-922-4NRA.

Before you buy a pistol and you are not familiar with hand-guns, take an NRA pistol course. Learn about the different types of pistols, how they work, the advantages and disadvantages of each design. Practice shooting the different types. Many ranges will, for a small fee, rent you pistols to shoot on the range.

Husbands, boyfriends and fathers who are themselves competent with firearms, often do not make the best instructors. Shooting and handling firearms for years or decades does not necessarily translate into being a good teacher for a beginner. *Call the NRA.*

Once you've made your mind up, be sure to remember to get cleaning gear, a holster appropriate for your method of carrying and any necessary strong box or lock for securing the pistol from unauthorized use. Also, get a box of full-power +P or +P+ *(Pronounced "plus P, plus P plus")* ammunition, along with 10 boxes of reloads for practice. Those ten boxes will give you 500 rounds to practice with, use them. The +P and +P+ designations have to do with the power of the ammunition with the +P being more powerful than standard .38 Special and +P+ yet again more powerful. Don't worry about a +P designation on .45 ACP they're all powerful enough to do the job. The current "Hot" ammunition is made by the Federal Cartridge Company and is called Hydra-Shok™. It is a rare occasion that a new defensive round is introduced without poor reviews in firearm's trade publications; but that is the case with Hydra-Shok™. In any event, use only name-brand ammunition similar to police-issue. If you have any doubts, ask your gun dealer.

A word about 9 mm automatics; I like the 9 mm and own three of them. For personal defense however, they are not as desirable as the .45 ACP (automatic colt pistol) cartridge. I was still involved in the military and bodyguard work when

I acquired my 9 mm pistols and occasionally accepted a task where there was a very real possibility of an armed confrontation with two or more men. Also, I've been shooting handguns since "Ike" was president, and I hit what I aim for. I often see Mr. & Mrs. middle-class in a gun store looking to buy a high-capacity 9 mm automatic for home defense. Poor choice, The odds of ever firing more than a couple of rounds in a home defense scenario are quite slim.

SHOTGUNS

Here again is the problem of people unfamiliar with firearms having to make choices due to their level of skill, willingness to seek training and become competent. For those with little desire to pursue adequate training I recommend a simple 12 or 20 gauge single barrel shotgun with the barrel cut to 18½ inches, recrowned, front sight reinstalled, a quick-detachable sling, and a buttstock shell holder. The finished product, if you start with a used shotgun, can be under $100.00. Any local gunsmith can read this paragraph and comply with it.

For those willing to invest a little time for training, the Mossberg Firearms Co. offers the "Home Security 410" a really neat little .410 gauge shotgun specifically designed for home defense, with a punch that exceeds the .44 Magnum. The optional laser sight is actually part of the shotgun, not stuck on the side. The intimidation factor of any shotgun is fantastic, but the added feature of a laser sight adds to this. When a person sees that red laser light on his chest there is no doubt in his mind or yours what the consequences of the gun being fired will be. That is precisely the message you want to convey.

PURCHASING YOUR FIREARM

Go to your local gun dealer, or locally owned sporting goods store. You may find the discount store is ten bucks cheaper. The last I heard Wal-Mart sells more guns than any store in the USA. You will also find the discount store clerk usually has very limited or no experience with firearms and can answer none of your questions. Your local gun dealer works on a profit margin so slim that most businessmen would regard the entire operation as unrealistic. Your gun dealer can answer all your questions, repair your gun and provide you with any accessory you would ever want.

TACTICS WITH FIREARMS IN THE HOME

As my wife can verify, a noise at 2:00 a.m. brings me to my feet, gun in hand, silently putting on trousers and shoes. I then go looking for the source of the noise.

As much as *experts* advocate the shotgun as the best home defense firearm, most people choose the handgun. To be useful the firearm must be loaded and must be quickly accessible. Children in the home make this difficult in that they must absolutely be trained not to ever touch a firearm without an adult being present. All other precautions are in *addition* to this basic one, not instead of it.

METAL BOXES

Gun stores sell metal boxes with combination locks for handguns. These boxes can be set so you need only push one button to unlock it.

CLOSET STORAGE

You can replace a closet door passageway lock with an outside entrance lock. The entrance way lock should fit with no new hole and possibly even utilize the same striker in the frame. Be sure the lock takes a different key than your others. Keep the door locked when gone, and unlocked when you need access to your firearms.

TRIGGER LOCKS
Trigger locks are too slow for your *ready gun*. They are well-suited for dead-storage. **CAUTION:** *Never Attempt To Install Or Remove A Trigger Lock From A Loaded And Cocked Firearm, It Can Discharge.*

GUN SAFES
Here you can spend from one hundred to several thousand dollars. Obviously, you get what you pay for, shop around, ask your gun dealer.

If there are no children about, your options are limitless. I have a friend who has many year's experience as a Special Forces Trooper. He keeps a loaded 12 gauge automatic shotgun hanging on the back of his bedroom door.

OTHER OPTIONS
Your gun store can sell you an inexpensive holster that you can fasten to a piece of $\frac{1}{4}$" plywood about the size of a legal pad. Attach the holster so that you can slip the plywood between your mattress and box spring with the holster hanging down next to your bed. A gun under your pillow can get uncomfortable or misplaced.

There are numerous attachments that mount flashlights to pistols and shotguns. Most gun stores can get what you need.

Laser sights are the hot item now. They are reliable, they're incredibly intimidating and not all that expensive anymore. A laser sight looks like a small flashlight; when properly attached to a firearm, will project a visible beam of red light, except in bright daylight. This beam is about the size of a pencil, it points precisely where the weapon will impact, if fired.

TRAINING
Don't just buy this equipment, put it in your closet and forget about it until you need it. Practice with your guns in the configuration you'll be using it in. Load and unload. Field strip, clean and reassemble. Dry fire and live fire. Twice a year minimum.

I practice shooting with both hands, I practice picking up an unloaded weapon, loading it and firing it as fast as I can. I practice shooting a hostile target half obscured by a hostage. I practice being surprised with my back facing the hostile. I practice shooting multiple targets at varying distances.

TACTICS WITH FIREARMS AWAY FROM HOME
Carrying a concealed weapon in most states requires a permit or special authorization. In most states it can be accomplished one way or another. Take the time, spend the money, do it right!

IN YOUR CAR
The pistol must be quickly accessible. Those little center consoles are ideal places. A door pocket is also handy. Don't leave your gun in the car! You're much more likely to be attacked away from your car than in it. Take your gun with you.

Public highway rest stops are dangerous places. Rest stops with no maintenance people around are particularly dangerous because you don't discover the danger until you're inside. Leave the car as a group, stay together, return to the car as a group. **Helpful Hint:** *Rapists sometimes hide inside the women's restroom.*

A popular highway robbery trick is for a decoy, usually a woman, to lie down on the side of the road late at night. You stop to help and the next thing you know you're being robbed by her boyfriend. Exercise caution around strangers and unusual situations.

Anytime you arrive at a roadside rest area, service station, restaurant, or motel and it "just doesn't feel right" trust your instinct and continue on to a better place.

NON-LETHAL WEAPONS

Tear-Gas is by far the most popular choice in this area. The best type is CS, a gas used by the military and police. This is some potent stuff. The first time I filled my lungs with it I was convinced I would die. The second time hurt, but I could function. The third incident slowed me down, but I kept on moving. You won't know if, or how many times a person has been hit by tear gas. Someone who has had experience with multiple doses, or is high enough on drugs may only get mad with a face full.

Pepper gas is rather new on the scene. It has Capsicum Red Pepper and is getting good reviews thus far. Tactics with it are the same as with tear-gas with slightly less chance of blow-back in your own face. Mace® now combines pepper in their gas.

Electric Stun-Guns are probably more effective, but you have to be close enough to touch the bad guy with it, which means he could more easily grab it from you.

Black-jacks, and nightsticks are quite effective in the hands of a trained person, as are all of the above mentioned weapons. Whatever weapon you choose, be absolutely sure you get adequate training for that weapon, and practice, practice, practice.

Most good-size communities have a law enforcement supply store catering to the needs of police officers. Gun stores, even if they don't stock these weapons, can order anything you need.

HOME DEFENSE AMMUNITION
Unless you live alone in a single family residence, keep in mind the problem of over-penetration. A .38 slug can go through two half-inch pieces of dry-wall and still seriously wound someone. The same holds true for full-power buckshot or slugs from a shotgun. The solution for pistols is the Glaser Safety Slug®. This round breaks up upon impact, greatly reducing the likelihood of over-penetration. For shotguns, BB shot will be less likely to over-penetrate than buckshot or slugs.

*****

ACTION ITEMS

1. If I decide to arm myself with a firearm, I will chose the one best suited to my needs and seek out an NRA qualified instructor. I will practice diligently.

2. I will learn and comply with all applicable laws concerning the purchase, possession, carrying concealed, transporting, and use of firearms where I live.

3. I will learn to properly use, care for, and store my firearms and ammunition so they will be secure from unauthorized use and ready for my use.

Chapter 9

CHILDREN'S SECURITY

"If you know the enemy and know yourself, your victory will not stand in doubt; if you know Heaven and know Earth, you may make your victory complete."
                                        —The Art of War, by Sun Tzu

*M*ost adults would agree that being a parent of a small child is a lot different today than it was only ten years ago. The media seems to have a never ending supply of horror stories about children being victims of crime. I find concerned neighbors and parents are always approaching my surveillance vehicle and inquiring as to my business in their neighborhood. These folks often cite small children in the area as the reason for their concern.

Following are some suggested guidelines:

1. When your children can understand, teach them to state their full name, home address and telephone number.

2. Never leave a child below the age of five unattended for even a minute.

3. Once a child can dial the telephone, teach them how to call for help by dialing the Operator. "911" is not available in all areas. As they get older, teach them how to make a collect-call home. I once was hired by an attorney to find his runaway daughter. The 14 year old called home two days later, explaining she did not know how to place a collect-call home. When your child matures upgrade his or her telephone training.

4. Each child, when away from home, should have a plastic-laminated ID Card in a pocket; not in a purse or backpack. Make it yourself using a piece of paper the size of a business card and list the child's name, home address, home phone, father's name and work phone, mother's name and work phone. Make up these cards ½ dozen at a time (cards get lost) and use plastic lamination. Still concerned? Sew in their name and home telephone number on their underwear.

5. Take a Red Cross first-aid course. Do it with your spouse and when your child is 12 or 13 years old, take it again with your child. I did and had a great time, my 13 year old daughter outscored four of the adults in the class on the written examination. Get a first-aid kit equal to your level of expertise. Better yet, get two kits, one for your vehicle, one for home.

6. Childhood should be a time of pleasant memories. Parents have a fine line to walk between giving their child the tools they need to be safe, and taking the fun out of being a kid. Children need to feel safe and feel loved. Shelter and protect them while peeling back the layers of the world's dangers as necessary and in a way that they still feel safe and in control.

7. Martial arts instruction for a pre-adolescent is a waste of resources. Once a child is five feet tall and weighs one hundred pounds, he or she is large enough to have some minimal martial arts instruction. Start with very simple moves to break the hold of an assailant so the child can escape. Progression from there depends on several factors such as, the child's desire, the perceived threat and resources available.

SELF-DEFENSE FOR SMALL CHILDREN

Running is the best defense for a small child. Teach the child to seek safety at a trusted neighbor's home or at an open store. The child should be taught how to speak up and ask for help. A recent twist used to lure a child into a stranger's car is to tell the child that his or her mother or father has been in an automobile accident; and the stranger has been asked to take the child to the injured parent. The abductor may even know the parent's name and place of employment and, of course, will address the child by name.

There is no limit to the ingenuity of criminals wishing to abduct children; so the basic rule of, *"never go anywhere with a stranger for any reason,"* must be repeated, every day if necessary.

I rarely see unaccompanied small children waiting for a school bus anymore. Children tend to be a bit more aware of their surroundings than in years past.

*****

ACTION ITEMS

1. I will follow the instructions of this chapter to assure my children's safety.

2. I will work with my children to make sure they are safe, but still remember they are kids who should enjoy the fun of childhood.

Chapter 10

COMBAT MINDSET

"The general who wins a battle makes many calculations in his temple before the battle is fought"
— The Art of War, by Sun Tzu

*T*his term describes the mindset of a person who has had training or experience that allows him or her to react instantly to a surprise attack with appropriate counter-force.

The mere use of the word combat will seem inappropriate to many people. However, if you speak to both victims of violent crime and veterans of combat, you will find their experiences more similar than different. The training necessary to become prepared for combat is closer to that which is required for self-protection. People who wish to attack you on the street or in your home rely on surprise to catch you unaware. They must get very close to you. Generally, not more than the length of a full-size car, (21 feet) before they can let you know they mean you harm; or enter your home without your knowledge. *You will have only seconds to recognize the threat, choose a course of action and retaliate.* Most people already have trained themselves in other areas to react quickly, following are some examples:

- ■ Drivers learn to react when they are confronted by an oncoming car that swerves into their lane by checking the right lane for an escape route. They check their rear view mirror for following traffic; then make their decision and act on it in a matter of seconds.

- ■ Tennis players learn from the sound of a ball being struck. They can tell the approximate velocity and the angle at which the ball is hit; and where they will have to run to intercept it. All of this happens in seconds with little time for deliberate thought.

- ■ Softball players learn to hit a pitched ball by instantly adjusting their swing to intercept the thrown ball. There is no time for a deliberate thought process here.

The above examples are common life-experiences to millions of people. They clearly show everyday use of being trained to respond in a proper manner to an instantly changing or surprise situation.

If you are willing to commit enough time you also can acquire a combat mindset. How much time should you commit to? That depends on who you are depending on your experiences and your needs.

Several years ago my wife, who was then my girlfriend, thought it would be funny to hide behind the refrigerator and jump out to surprise me. I walked into what I thought was an empty kitchen and caught movement out of the corner of my eye as I passed the refrigerator. I caught myself before striking her a defensive blow. I then cautioned her never to consider a similar "surprise" again, because I could have harmed her.

Here we have a proper, controlled response, not being caught "off guard," or responding with an out-of-control reaction.

Criminals rely on their ability to surprise you and paralyze you with fear before you can react. They practice the art of deception. They will stop you to ask for the time of day, directions, spare change or any ploy to get close enough to distract you before their display of a weapon. Most intended victims react in such a predictable manner! They freeze, they do what they're told, they give up their property, their dignity and all too often their lives.

How many times have you read an account of a crime where the victim's first words are "It happened so fast." Of course it happened fast! I hope that you see value in having a combat mindset as part of your self-protection skills. How does one acquire these skills? Here are some ideas.

The rapidly growing sport of paint-ball combat matches can offer; with modification, training opportunities such as:

1. Stage a scenario where you take a walk and are approached by six different men at different points. All of these men look like good citizens; one is a bad guy. He will attempt to attack you.

2. Pretend to be asleep in a cabin that is being broken into.

3. Be in a car at a stop light that comes under attack.

You can practice these scenarios in your home with a *toy* pistol.

The acquisition of a combat mindset is an evolution coming from learning the skills and habits discussed in other chapters.

These are: learning the threat, acquiring a positive mental attitude, learning the law on deadly force in your area, preparing your home and car against crime, learning martial arts and firearms handling, and buying a firearm.

Learning them to the point that they become part of you. Practicing these skills on an ongoing basis. Keeping your mind clear and focused, keeping your equipment clean and ready for use. *You can do it!*

*****

ACTION ITEMS

1. I will acquire a proper combat mindset and make it part of my being.

2. I will not be a victim of crime.

3. I will prevail if someone attacks me.

4. I will constantly improve my skills and become a more confident prepared individual; and will be ready to take care of myself.

Chapter 11

SEXUAL ASSAULT

"Walk in the path defined by rule, and accommodate yourself to the enemy until you can fight a decisive battle. At first then, exhibit the coyness of a maiden, until the enemy gives you an opening; afterward emulate the rapidity of a running hare, and it will be too late for the enemy to oppose you."
—The Art of War, by Sun Tzu

I was shocked at the response to my questions asking women about their concerns in this area. What really surprised me was the level of concern regarding acquaintance rape. It is doubtlessly true that women have for centuries submitted to sexual assault due to the position or power of the attacker.

My first wife was raped by a superior at work. He was an MD and psychiatrist. He told her that reporting the rape would be futile, which it probably would have (especially in 1974). She refused to tell me for fear I would take action. The perpetrator went free on that one.

Learn to trust your instinct about acquaintances. Act on your instinct. If you feel "uncomfortable" about being alone with a man, don't allow yourself to be alone with him. If for reasons seemingly beyond your control you have to be alone with a man you are uncomfortable with, *be prepared to defend yourself immediately with all force necessary to end an attack.* For most men, the fear of being found out to be a rapist will quell them before the attack gets beyond your verbal demand that they stop.

You must make a very clear, concise verbal demand that he stop his advances. Men can often be incredible clods and really believe you want them sexually when you want nothing of the sort. *Be firm, be clear, do not allow any unwanted touching, defend yourself.* If you submit to a single kiss or caress, thinking that you can stop him at some later point you will not only be encouraging the man's sexual desires; you will destroy your credibility as a victim in a court of law.

This may sound harsh, but I believe it is accurate and good advice. The recent case of William Kennedy Smith in Florida is a good example of a woman losing credibility by her actions. Up to the moment of the actual lovemaking or sexual assault, the victim had conducted herself as agreeable and willing participant in a casual sexual encounter. After an evening of drinking, rubbing against and kissing Kennedy, she finally escorted him to his home in the middle of the night, rather than dropping him off and going home to her child.

In our system of justice, guilt must be established "beyond reasonable doubt." It would be very hard to find a jury that would unanimously convict Kennedy given the fact situation. *Had the victim either been injured or injured Kennedy while defending herself, she would have had a much more credible story.*

Defend yourself with all you have. Defend with your heart, your soul; scream, punch, kick, bite; never submit. A little Pepper Mace® in the face wouldn't hurt either.

If you use deadly force against an unarmed acquaintance intent on raping you, and you kill him, my prayers are with you. Review Chapter 3 on the use of deadly force. Then review it a second time. The law generally expects deadly force to be used only against deadly force.

If you are five feet tall and weigh one-hundred pounds, a man six feet tall and over twice your weight could constitute deadly force over you. A lawyer can make this argument for you. Your best tactic is to let your lawyer defend you if you find yourself in this situation.

Of course, the preferable course of action is to avoid this scenario altogether. A face full of Pepper Mace® will dampen the lust of most men in a hurry.

*****

ACTION ITEMS

1. I will learn to trust and act on my instincts about acquaintances.

2. I will be firm in letting someone know I want him to stop his advances.

3. If I am attacked, I will resist with all force necessary; my heart, my soul, my very being. *I will never submit.*

Chapter 12

TIPS FOR BUSINESS AND VACATION TRAVELERS

"Raising a host of a hundred thousand men and marching them great distances entails heavy loss on the people and a drain on the resources of the state. The daily expenditure will amount to a thousand ounces of silver. There will be commotion at home and abroad and men will drop down exhausted on the highways."

—The Art of War, by Sun Tzu

*G*oing on trips means leaving our familiar surroundings for places we generally have less knowledge of; which causes potential security concerns for us. Most people traveling alone on a business trip compensate for this by being more vigilant than usual.

Those on vacation may become lax in their normal awareness as part of a general "winding down" attitude.

The advice offered throughout this book should be applied in these scenarios with the following additional thoughts:

FOR THE BUSINESS TRAVELER
1. Do not use any public transportation such as buses or subways.

2. Do not walk in any downtown area of any major city after dark, unless you are prepared to defend yourself against armed assault.

3. Don't wear flashy, expensive looking jewelry or flashy clothes, if you will be in areas accessible to the public.

4. If you elect to arm yourself on your trip; before your visit, find out what the local laws are concerning this and comply with them.

5. As soon as you "feel" yourself being "sized-up" by a bad guy, take immediate action to neutralize the threat. Retreat to a place where there are people; and get help. Don't be concerned about what impression you make when expressing your need for help; just do it.

6. Select a hotel that has everything you need under one roof. This will drastically reduce your exposure. This also may mean a higher cost to your company, but you are worth it. These concerns should be respected by your company without criticism.

FOR THE VACATIONER
1. Traveling with children presents a whole set of unique problems. Many popular tourist attractions (Grand Canyon, dams, waterfalls) are extremely dangerous. *Failure of children to obey the adults can have tragic results.* Practice exercising discipline before the trip by visiting your local

attractions. Avoid dangerous areas if you feel uneasy about not having control of your children.

2. One person shall be the leader to whom everybody reports where they will always be.

3. No child under age 13 should be unescorted in an uncontrolled public area. This excludes theme parks for younger children, depending on maturity.

4. Kick back, relax, but maintain a level of security awareness appropriate for where you are.

5. The downtown areas of most major US cities are dangerous places, day or night. Do not use public transportation. Avoid isolated locations. Quickly move on at the first hint of a confrontation.

6. If you elect to arm yourself, find out what the local laws are before your visit and comply with them.

7. In places like Washington DC the armed criminal is virtually guaranteed unarmed victims. Do what you must, to be secure. (travel only in large groups, hire a squad of Marines)

8. Specialty luggage shops sell small cloth wallets designed to hang from the neck, under your clothing. These are a great place for your passport, extra cash, and a piece of paper listing all your credit cards, card company telephones and other important telephone numbers. *DON'T TAKE YOUR WALLET OUT IN PUBLIC!* Rather go to a private place to remove or replace something.

9. Traveler checks should not be counter-signed until the moment you use them.

10. If you want to reduce your exposure, don't look like a tourist; that is, don't walk around with a camera around your neck. Don't carry many packages. Unload them at your room, or rent a locker. Don't wear funny hats or shorts, unless the locals do.

*****

ACTION ITEMS

1. I will review these tips and make them part of my travel plans.

2. I will keep security awareness in mind when traveling.

Chapter 13

CIVIL DISORDER PREPARATION

"There are five ways of attacking with fire. The first is to burn soldiers in their camp; the second is to burn stores; the third is to burn baggage trains; the fourth is to burn arsenals and magazines; the fifth is to hurl dropping fire among the enemy."
—The Art of War, by Sun Tzu

*C*ivil disorder is combat. The enemy is anyone attempting to destroy life or property. The preparations you make now will be what you use when a crisis occurs.

The recurring theme throughout this book stresses that you should take responsibility for your personal and family's protection. The threat of civil disorder exists in many major metropolitan areas. Even tiny Warrensburg Missouri (population 13,800 and many miles from a major metropolitan area) had a riot following the Rodney King verdict that destroyed a number of its small downtown businesses.

You prepare for civil disorder much as you should for an earthquake or blackout. Plan to meet all of your family's needs for two weeks. Be independent of the power grid, telephone service (except cellular which has proved to be more reliable), natural gas, water, sewer, fire and police protection.

CRISIS PREPLANNING
Along with everything in the *preceding* chapters:

1. Check with your Insurance agent to determine coverage for a loss due to civil disorder. Business owners should have "interruption of business" coverage. If it is cost prohibitive, you are faced with having to defend your business, losing everything you own, sell it or move it now.

2. Develop a complete family plan with every family member knowing what their responsibility is. Every part of the plan should have at least two backup contingencies: *For example, Mom gets Suzy from school: 1. By car, 2. Ride bicycle, or, 3. Walk.*

3. Work with your neighborhood watch group to develop plans for any emergency such as earthquakes or civil disorder. As with the family plan everyone should know their responsibility and every part of the plan should have at least two back-up contingencies. A group leader should be elected. This is combat and decisions cannot be made by committee.

4. Suggested group tasks:
    a. security and defense
    b. first-aid
    c. food preparation and acquisition
    d. sanitation
    e. communication and intelligence
    f. child care
    g. transportation

5. A commercial quality bullhorn should be acquired. You can warn off looters from a distance advising that you are armed and ready. You can let police know who you are. You can alert others in your group.

6. The best defensive weapons for these situations are:

a. 12 gauge shotguns

b. major caliber rifles. (any rifle legal to hunt deer) Consult with your local gun shop for what will fit your needs and budget.

7. See *Recommended Reading* section of this book.

CRISIS MANAGEMENT

Once "the balloon goes up" and you find yourself in the middle of a major disruption:

1. Keep a cool head. Think out your situation, act as calmly and deliberately as possible.

2. Every situation will be different calling for common-sense judgments to be made with little information to go on.

3. Your two basic options are to:
   A. Tough it out at home
   B. Retreat to a safe area

Most choose "A" for as long as it makes sense. The threat of a fire storm may make decision "B" for you.

4. Have all valuables pre-packed for immediate evacuation or bury them in your back yard.

5. Fly The Colors and display the American Flag prominently. Make a sign offering coffee to police and guardsmen.

*****

ACTION ITEMS

1. I will develop a family plan immediately, by _____

2. I will urge my neighborhood watch group to plan for civil disorder, earthquakes, blackouts.

3. I will acquire all the material items and training I will need by _____ so my family will be ready.

CONCLUSION

"He will win who, (sic) prepared himself, waits to take the enemy unprepared."
                                        —The Art of War, by Sun Tzu

You have just finished reading one of the best books available on how and where to learn everything you need to know in order not to be a passive victim of crime.

So far as personal security preparedness is concerned there are two extremes when describing individuals. At one extreme are those who are so consumed with fear that they severely curtail their activities. The opposite extreme are those totally oblivious to any danger. Most people fall somewhere in between, with the majority making some conscious effort to lock the doors of their home and car, not traveling to certain "bad" parts of town alone or at night, not carrying large amounts of cash and having proper insurance. The premise of this book has been to first demonstrate that most individuals have a distorted sense of what the dangers really are, and second, that the generally accepted levels of passive preparedness mentioned above are totally inadequate. I believe at this point it should be mentioned that most government agencies and most mass-media accounts suggest using passive methods of preparedness, telling you not to resist.

My goal has been to present a comprehensive plan to take the offense in protecting yourself and your family. Passive security methods may once have been proper, but those who use them now all too often become victims. *The time to implement your personal security plan is now, prior to you needing it.* The more quickly and better prepared you become now, the less likely you will become a victim of crime in the future.

Many who have read this book have expressed concern about the suggested use of firearms and deadly force. I regard these items as only part, albeit an important part, of your comprehensive personal security planning. The use of deadly force is not "The" answer, but rather "Part of" the answer to be implemented at the conclusion of every other aspect of your security planning having failed first.

When times are tough, the tough get going!

Just do it!

Get tough!

Get going!

GLOSSARY

.45 A.C.P.: The standard US Army pistol caliber from 1911 to the 1980s when the 9 mm parabellum became standard. Special operations in the military still prefer the .45 ACP for its one-shot-stop capabilities.

A.C.P.: Abbreviation for Automatic Colt Pistol, used to designate several types of pistol cartridges developed by Colt Firearms.

Automatic Pistol: A term usually used to describe a semi-automatic pistol. Also referred to as a self-loading pistol these pistols fire once each time the trigger is squeezed and usually stores the ammunition in a removable magazine.

Blackjack (leather slapper): A police weapon made of leather and eight to eleven inches long with lead in the end for more impact.

Body-armor: Often mistakenly called bulletproof vest, there is no such thing as a "bulletproof" vest. Modern lightweight body armor will stop most common pistol bullets. Sold by police supply stores and some gun stores by special order, they can be a real lifesaver if you spend much time in a high-crime area.

Caliber: Describes the type of ammunition used in a rifle or pistol. US calibers are based on the width of the bullet measured in hundredths of an inch. For example: .45 ACP is a bullet .45/100ths of an inch wide. European calibers measure the width of the bullet in millimeters. For example: 9 mm is a bullet that is 9 millimeters wide.

Combat: A fight between individuals or groups.

Crack Cocaine: A concentrated form of cocaine that looks like small white rocks. When smoked, gives an instant very intense high. Can induce an instant heart attack.

Electric Stun-Gun: A small hand-held weapon that will deliver a painful, sometimes paralyzing jolt of electricity to an attacker. Battery operated; there are many types with varying degrees of effectiveness.

Gauge: The inside diameter of a shotgun barrel as determined by the number of equal size lead balls, one of which is same size as the diameter of the barrel. For example a 12 gauge shotgun has a barrel diameter equal to a one twelfth pound lead ball.

Groundfire: In war, the firing of weapons at aircraft from the ground.

Methamphetamine: A prescription drug; street name, Speed. Legal use: to control attacks of uncontrollable sleepiness, or hyperactivity in children; Criminal Use: Induces a feeling of being "high," rapid heartbeat, hyperactivity, hallucinations, suicidal or homicidal feelings.

Mortar: A small man-portable indirect-fire weapon that shoots a small rocket containing high-explosives up to several miles away.

National Rifle Association (NRA): the oldest and largest group dedicated to the shooting sports. One stop shopping for training, education, books, and legislative influence. Call 1-800-922-4NRA.

Nightstick: A police weapon usually made of hardwood or plastic 16 to 26 inches long and 1 inch in diameter. Proper training in its use is necessary.

PCP: Street Name: Angel Dust; Horse tranquilizer, makes you high, makes you crazy.

Performance Bond: A type of insurance that will pay off in the event the person or company "bonded" fails to perform. For example, a bonded construction company protects their customers against defective materials or workmanship by offering a performance bond to them guaranteeing same.

Rocket: In current battlefield tactics a small man-portable line-of-sight weapon that fires a rocket projectile several hundred yards.

Revolver: A pistol that fires once each time the trigger is squeezed (double action revolver) or will fire once after the hammer is cocked (single action revolver). The ammunition is stored in a cylinder that "revolves."

Snipe: To shoot (usually with a high-powered rifle) at exposed individuals of an enemy's forces, especially when not in action from a concealed vantage position.

Sports Car Club of America (SCCA): The sanctioning group for amateur car racing. Learn to drive, really drive 1-800-255-5550.

Submachine Gun: A full-automatic weapon that uses pistol ammunition and fires continuously when the trigger is depressed until the trigger is released or the ammunition is expended.

World War Two (WWII): The major conflict of the twentieth century 1939-1945.

ABOUT THE AUTHOR

Mr. Moore is a veteran of the Vietnam War where he flew as a crew member on 57 combat missions, many of which resulted in his aircraft being hit by enemy ground fire. During his main job of conducting intelligence studies in Vietnam he was a courier of classified documents and large amounts of cash. His daily routine included the morning search for a terrorist bomb in his jeep, being the target of snipers, evenings of mortar attacks, rocket attacks and patrolling alleys at night alone.

Graduating from college as a legal assistant, Mr. Moore became a private detective in 1973.

His career has included being a criminal investigator for the State of Missouri where he went alone looking for and finding murderers. He has had bodyguard assignments both in the military and as a private bodyguard. His work on the street includes conducting surveillances in high-crime areas and pursuit driving every working day for years.

He has instructed rookie investigators in the art of criminal investigations, surveillance techniques, pursuit driving and is an NRA Certified firearm's instructor.

Mr. Moore has lived "on the edge" since 1967 and has acquired a deep understanding of what works and what does not work in personal security. His decision to go public with his knowledge is helping many to lead less stressful, more productive lives.

PRODUCT AND SERVICES

LIFE AND CRIME IN AMERICA:
You Can Protect Your Family

John Moore will speak to your group or company. His presentation *"Life And Crime In America: You Can Protect Your Family"* will give everyone who attends information they need; information suppressed by the mainstream media.

Call (314) 965-3007 for more information

For additional copies of:

FEEL SAFE ANYWHERE:
You Can Be Your Own Bodyguard

(Quantity Discounts Available)

ENCLOSED IS $12.50 PER BOOK
($10.00 plus $2.50 shipping per book)

(Money Order or Check)

Please mail _____ copies to:

Name_____

Address_____

City _____State_____ Zip _____

FOR MORE INFORMATION CONTACT:

Tiger Enterprises
Attn: "J. R." Moore
PO Box 9901
Kirkwood, Missouri 63122
(314) 965-3007

RECOMMENDED READINGS AND SOURCES

READINGS
To Ride, Shoot Straight, and Speak The Truth, by Jeff Cooper. Cooper's crisp style covers a lot of ground from secure home designs to combat mindset.

Dead Clients Don't Pay: The Bodyguard's Manual, by Leroy Thompson.
A look at how the pros do it.

In The Gravest Extreme: The role of the firearm in personal protection, by Massad Ayoob.
This book goes into depth on preparation, tactics, and the legal aftermath of a shooting.

Survival Guns, by Mel Tappen.
Mr. Tappen's classic work on what firearms are best suited for what mission.

SOURCES
Lancer Militaria • Books, Videos and Military Manuals
P.O. Box 886
Mt. Ida, AR 71957
(501) 867-2232
(501) 867-3431 FAX

Delta Press Ltd. • Books and Military Manuals
P.O. Box 1625
El Dorado, AR 71730
(501) 862-4984
(501) 862-9671 FAX

Brigade Quartermasters • Self-Defense Equipment and
Survival Supplies
1025 Cobb International Blvd.
Kennesaw, GA 30144-4300
(404) 428-1234
(404)-426-8504 FAX

Paladin Press • Books and Military Manuals
P.O. Box 1307
Boulder, CO 80306
(303) 443-7250
(303) 442-8741 FAX

U.S. Cavalry • Self-Defense Equipment, Survival Supplies
2855 Centennial Ave
Radcliff, KY 40160-9000
(502) 351-1164
(502) 352-0266 FAX

Shomer-Tec • Law Enforcement and Military Equipment
P.0. Box 2039
Bellingham, WA 98227
(206) 733-6214
(206) 676-5248 FAX

Diebold • Commercial Quality High Security Doors, Safes,
Access Systems, Closed Circuit, TV, and Alarms
P.O. Box 8230
Canton, OH 44711- 8230
(216) 489-4000
(216) 489-4104 FAX

National Rifle Association • Firearms Training, Information,
Political help on anti-gun laws
1600 Rhode Island Avenue, NW
Washington D.C. 20036-3268
1-800-538-4NRA